let's colour

sports colouring book 1

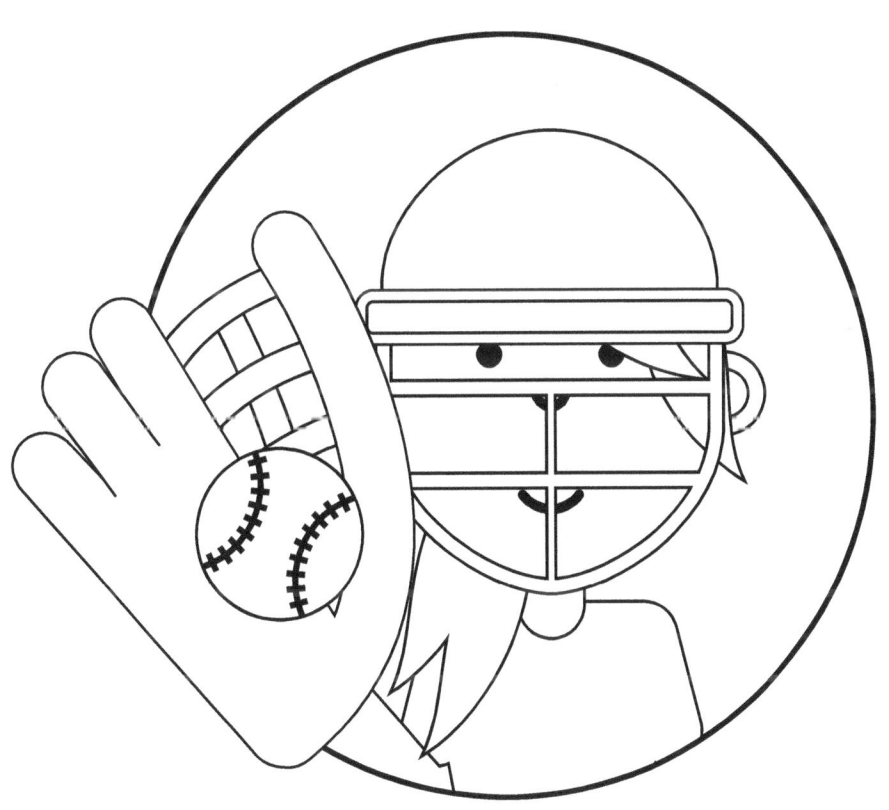

Thank you to the coaches and SMAC® team members for believing in this project and to my friends and family. A special thanks to contributors Dean, Jasmine and Robyn.

Let's Colour Sports Colouring Book 1
ISBN 978-0-6481963-3-4
Copyright © 2020 John Connelly. All rights reserved.
Design by John Connelly
Illustrations by Dean Lahn, John Connelly & Robyn Souphandavong
Editing by John Connelly
First Published in Australia 2020 by SMAC®

www.movingwell.org
Moving Well Foundation Edition
'Moving well is living well' ™

let's colour

sports colouring book 1

by John Connelly

Hi, I'm..
....

I like to play...
....

with..
....

Softball

Cricket

Soccer

Coach Karen

Coach John

Time to choose which team to join! Do you want to be on Coach Karen and Charlie's team? Draw yourself and a friend here.

Come on! Let's meet!

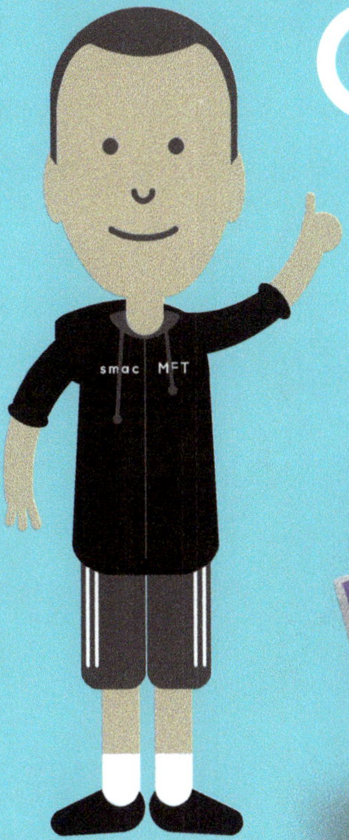

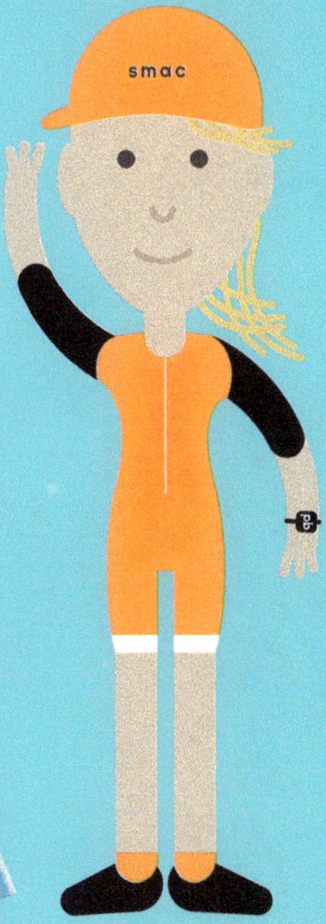

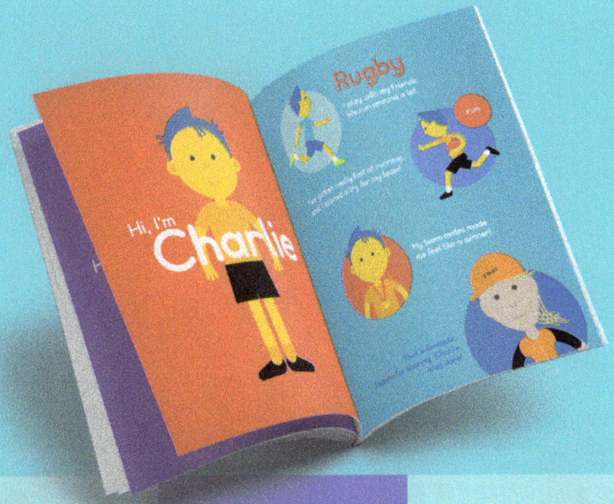

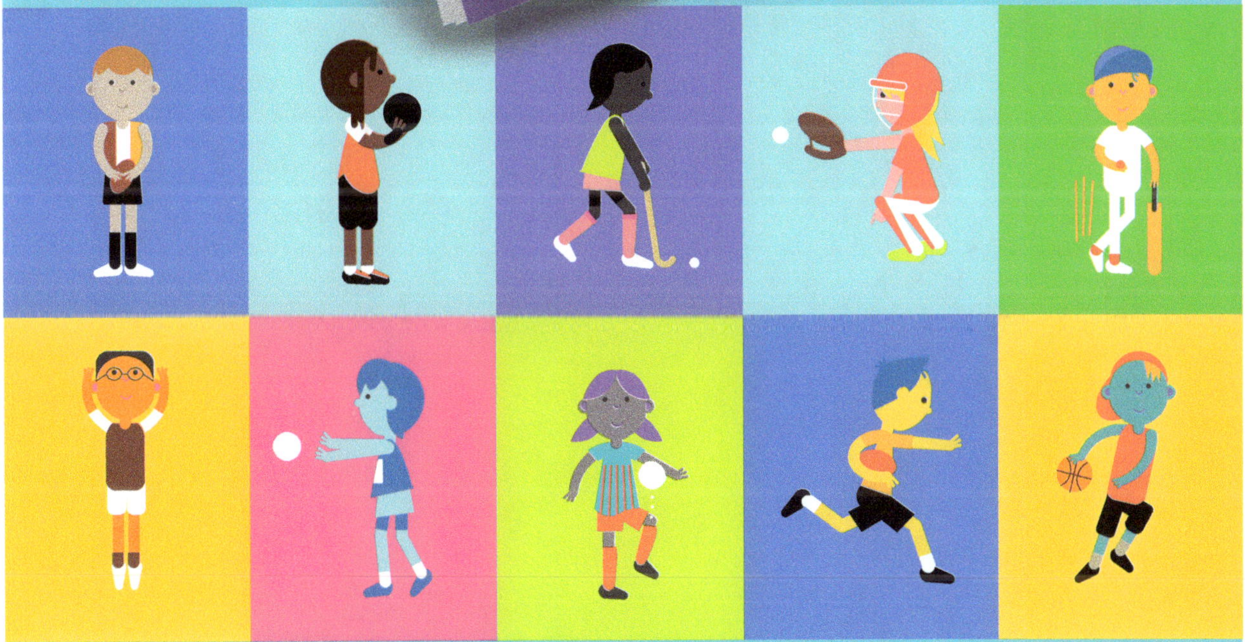

let's colour

www.movingwell.org

let's move

www.ingramcontent.com/pod-product-compliance
Lightning Source LLC
Chambersburg PA
CBHW061135010526
44107CB00068B/2947